WEALTH SECRETS THE RICH WON'T TELL YOU

The No-Fail System for Easily Building Long-Term Wealth

Denise J. Whalen

Denise J. Whalen

Copyright © 2022 Denise J. Whalen

All rights reserved.

ISBN: 9798845945990

Disclaimer

This book in no way constitutes professional or financial advice. Take what I say in this book as my subjective assessment and assessment based on current economic trends and fundamental measures I've taken personally.

You are accountable for your actions if you act on the ideas or opinions expressed in this book.

Denise J. Whalen

Table of Contents

Disclaimer 3
Table of Contents 4
INTRODUCTION 6
Chapter ONE 8
   What Exactly Is "Wealth-Building?" 8
Chapter TWO 18
   The Eight Wealth-Building Commandments 18
Chapter THREE 28
   Wealth-Building Mistakes to Avoid 28
Chapter FOUR 38
   Long-Term Wealth Development Strategies 38
Chapter FIVE 46
   What exactly is generational wealth? 46
Chapter SIX 56
   Ways of Building Wealth from Scratch 56
BONUS 66
   Passive Income Ideas for Future Wealth 66
Conclusion 74

Wealth Secrets The Rich Won't Tell You

Denise J. Whalen

INTRODUCTION

The phrase "generational wealth" is a popular and well-known topic that virtually every adult has heard at one point in time, either on social media platforms or offline. However, you might well have put it to the subconscious mind since you have more important concerns. Learning to create riches from nothing may feel like a "mission impossible," especially if you've always assumed that wealthy individuals inherited their fortune or benefited from significant connections.

If you can leave something some sort of property behind for your offspring or grandkids, you are helping to increase your family's generational wealth. However, I'm talking about the financial riches you're able to leave behind.

This wealth can take numerous forms, such as future financial education, real estate holdings, and stock market investments. People frequently question why the wealthy continue to amass wealth. Is there some secret sauce that allows the wealthy to continue to increase their fortune yearly while the typical person struggles to pay their debts and save for retirement?

Building wealth is a topic that may stir intense debate, encourage bizarre get-rich-quick scams, or push individuals to engage in activities they would never consider otherwise. As we all know, accumulating wealth is a time-consuming process. Although the prospect of being an overnight billionaire appeals to many people, the only way to get wealthy overnight is through speculation, inheritance, or a lottery win.

Building wealth might be intimidating when you're beginning from scratch. But don't worry; there are a wide range of options. And, with a little hard work, you can well be on your way to gaining independence financially in no time.

This book is just a guide to the countless measures anyone can take to get a head start and build long-term wealth.

Chapter ONE

What Exactly Is "Wealth-Building?"

Wealth building is creating long-term income from various sources, such as income-generating assets, savings, or other investments. The notion of wealth creation is based on knowledge and appropriate financial planning for one's future financial aspirations. Many people will resort to wealth creation to guarantee a strong financial future.

What Are the Best Assets for Building Wealth?

Certain retirement accounts, real estate, equities, and private notes backed by real estate have traditionally been the finest wealth-building assets because each asset can create a constant flow of cash. On the other hand, the other assets have the ability to generate returns for clever investors, and are believed to be among the best.

Annuities, mutual funds, CDs, bonds, and other wealth-building instruments are also available.

According to one financial approach, "the best wealth-building assets investors should possess are stocks/equities since they have strong historical returns." They are simple to own and trade, and they require little care.

Bonds are another good option since they are less volatile. They are beneficial for rebalancing and, in theory, safe." While certain wealth-building assets are seen to be more high-yielding than others, each possibility will have drawbacks. Continue reading to discover more about the finest wealth-building assets and the advantages and disadvantages of each technique.

1. Retirement Plans:

Retirement funds, particularly 401(k) and Roth IRA accounts, may be excellent assets for accumulating wealth. There is, however, a catch: you are unable to make use of the funds until the moment you attain retirement age. While these solutions may not increase your monthly income immediately, they will offer you a more secure financial future.

A 401(k) is a contributing retirement plan available to employees through their companies. Some firms may even match contributions to a specific level, giving employees free money for the future. Contributions are tax-deferred until withdrawn and can accumulate significantly over time.

A Roth IRA is another retirement choice, but you can open one without the help of your employer. The contribution maximum is now $6,000 for filers under the age of 50 and $7,000 for taxpayers over the age of 50. Again, you cannot access the assets until retirement, but this is an excellent strategy to accumulate wealth over time. Retirement funds may not be as exciting as stocks or real estate, but they are essential assets for future planning.

2. Real Estate:

Probably one of the best wealth-creating investments in real estate. Throughout the years, real estate has proven to be a profitable investment opportunity for people who know what they're doing. According to research, the average rate of return for real estate during 150 years was about 8%. Stocks were the second best performing asset, with a 7% average return rate. Other wealth-building investments, such as CDs and bonds, averaged less than 3%.

The excellent performance of real estate is due to several variables, including the opportunity for monthly cash flow through rental revenue and a large number of tax benefits available to investors. Those interested in real estate must select the appropriate property type and exit plan.

Begin by analyzing your target market and determining which locations have the greatest potential. Residential real estate, commercial buildings, and unoccupied land are all possibilities. While residential real estate entails techniques such as renting out vacation homes or house hacking, commercial real estate can be appealing due to long-term leases and financial possibilities.

Investing in real estate to build wealth is an appealing prospect for anybody seeking long-term financial security. Many businesses will discover that they may reinvest a portion of their income and increase their portfolios since real estate can offer steady cash flow. There are various methods to reinvest the profits from real estate investing, including buying other homes or investing in other wealth-building assets.

3. Stocks:

Another well-known example of a wealth asset is publicly traded equities. Stocks provide investors with the option to purchase shares in firms and benefit from them. Over time, stocks have shown to be a powerful wealth-building instrument. As previously said, several studies demonstrate that stocks are a highly profitable investment, with a rate of return average of approximately 7%. Stocks are a popular long-term investment for many investors; however, they may be volatile soon.

Compared to other wealth-building investments, many investors will discover that publicly traded equities may provide a kind of diversification. Stocks can help entrepreneurs who have had success with other investing techniques increase their profit margins.

4. Real Estate-Secured Private Notes:

Real estate notes are convertible notes that ensure the repayment of a loan or mortgage. They allow investors to serve as lenders rather than actively engage in real estate. Because they allow investors to take a more passive role, private notes are an appealing tool for accumulating wealth through real estate. To be successful, this method does need some prior knowledge. As a result, investors should conduct a thorough investigation before getting started.

There are three types of private notes to be aware of: loans for rehabbing houses, seller-financed notes, and loans for homeowners. Fix, and flip loans often have high-interest rates for a short period, ranging from six to twelve months on average. If lenders know what to expect, notes for seller-financed houses can be beneficial.

Before looking at this possibility, ensure you're familiar with seller financing. Finally, investors can serve as lenders for ordinary homeowners. This simple approach entails serving as a lender for prospective homebuyers.

Investors must have a borrowers screening procedure when engaging with individual notes. Consider the loan-to-value (LTV) ratio and the borrower's debt-to-income ratio. When handled properly, private notes may be a beneficial investment; nevertheless, investors should comprehend the structure before becoming completely engaged.

The Three Steps to Wealth Creation

Before you start thinking of investing your money, you must possess at least two to four consistent income sources guaranteed to last the duration of your life time. Establishing a solid savings strategy is recommended before any form of investment can begin. Finally, the moment has come to invest.

To accumulate money over time, you must do three easy steps:

- Invest money
- Save money
- Earn money

1. Investing Money:

Finally, you may begin investing your money once you've established a solid basis. However, to establish a broad investment portfolio, you must be willing to accept certain risks. It is critical to investigate how much asset allocation is acceptable for you.

While you may conduct this research on your own, it is also suggested that novice investors consult with a financial professional. They can assist you in determining your risk tolerance, investment objectives, and time horizon. Based on these insights, they may assist you in developing a balanced portfolio that is risk-averse, moderate, or aggressive, depending on your preferences.

It's worth noting that there are various beginner-friendly Robo-advisors and investing apps available.

2. Saving Money:

Setting aside a specific percentage of your income on a regular basis is the second element to building long-lasting wealth. It's a common trend that most people don't have adequate savings, yet live luxurious lifestyles after gaining momentary financial security. It would be best for you to focus on generating passive income by investing, especially once you've saved a considerable amount of money. Here are some simple methods to begin saving money:

- Contribute to your retirement plan. Take advantage of any matching plans offered by your work. Do not throw away free money.
- Keep around six months' worth of costs on hand in an emergency. Having a buffer can assist you in avoiding derailing your finances whenever something unexpected occurs.

- Adjust your budget as you experiment to the point where you're saving money every month but without starving yourself to the point where living is no longer fun.
- Keep track of your monthly expenditure, and then eliminate the products, services, and experiences you don't truly require.

3. Making Money:

This stage may appear apparent, but it is critical to emphasize that a consistent source of solid income over time is critical to wealth creation. A tiny amount of consistent savings from this source of income might add up to a sizable sum.

A key topic to put into consideration is whether your current job can provide you with a consistent amount of savings for the next 35 to 45 years. If not, it may be time to seek other strategies or approaches to boosting your overall earnings and income. As we all know, passive and earned income are the two main avenues of generating income. Passive income comes mainly from investments while earned income is the money obtained from your regular job.

To boost your earnings, you may need to alter your occupation first. If you're thinking about changing careers, ask yourself some questions to help you decide. What do you love doing, and what talents do you naturally possess?

Finding a career matching your strengths and tasks that you like will automatically help you perform better and increase your income. Of course, it's your duty to ensure that your chosen profession pays well. Hence, you should consider investing money in your education and other trainings to enable you become a more competitive applicant for the job you want.

Once you've established adequate financial stability, you may begin saving and investing.

Chapter TWO

The Eight Wealth-Building Commandments

True wealth entails far more than simply increasing your economic value. Yes, financial independence is all about money, but so is living a prosperous life. This difference is important. We've all seen affluent folks who are happy and impoverished people who are unhappy.

According to research, the association between money and happiness is insignificant. The fundamental eight principles outlined below will assist you in achieving genuine prosperity – both personally and financially.

First Principle: Be Extremely Motivated.

Money is a superficial incentive – much too shallow to propel you to success. The issue is that financial riches are an external objective with advantages restricted to the world around you. Money can't buy pleasure, even though it can very well buy other material things. It can make your jail look nicer but can't get you out.

The intrinsic restrictions of external ambitions (expensive mansions, vehicles, and large money accounts) limit your motivation to pursue them. To be successful in accumulating riches, you must be motivated by internal ambitions that go beyond the external trappings of wealth.

You desire a cause that will improve your life and motivate you to conquer all the barriers on your way to financial freedom. Internally motivated goals that may hold your attention long enough for you to succeed include the following:

1. **Leadership**: Grow your money joyfully and ethically so that you may set a good example for family and friends who want to break free from the constraints of financial mediocrity and follow in your footsteps.

2. **Personal Development**: You tend to have ample time to chase personal freedom when you gain financial independence. The riches in your exterior environment reflect the prosperity in your inner life. The concepts that lead to financial riches can also lead to genuine wealth by impacting other aspects of your life.

3. **Charitable Giving**: When you have more you, then you can offer more. Wealthy families' charitable foundations frequently give the financial strength to support important social and environmental initiatives.

4. **Freedom**: Break free from the chains of everyday labor so you may devote more time to growing, creating, and living to your full potential.

Deeper causes are important since accumulating money is difficult. Along the way to financial independence, you will face several challenges you must conquer to achieve your goal. You have to possess drive and stay on course to succeed. This step-by-step guide to financial independence will assist you in discovering your "why" and propelling you toward your objective.

Second Principle: Give More Than You Take.

Giving more than you receive reflects on everyone and makes them better off. That is how genuine wealth is created. You enhance the lives of others by improving your own. Sure, many people throughout history built financial empires by abusing others or the environment, but stealing value will never lead to pleasure or contentment. Exploitation may yield money, but delivering value also offers satisfaction and fulfillment – genuine wealth. The wealthier you get, the more you give to others. And it's a fulfilling way to live.

Third Principle: Build Wealth Using Leverage.

Leverage is a critical success element for accumulating money. You will not get wealthy by exchanging time for money, and you cannot accomplish everything alone. Building money necessitates working smarter rather than harder by employing the following leveraging principles:

1. **Leveraging Knowledge**: Leveraging the experience, expertise, and abilities of others allows you to use more knowledge than you can ever have.

2. **Leveraging the Power of Network**: Leveraging the relationships and resources of others allows you to go beyond your own.

3. **Leveraging the Art of Marketing**: Using other people's databases, periodicals, radio shows, and newsletters allows you to reach millions of individuals without effort.

4. **Leveraging Systems and Technology**: Using other people's technologies and methods allows you to do more with less effort.

5. **Leveraging Time**: Using other people's time to avoid being constrained to 24 hours a day.

6. **Financial Leverage**: Using other people's money to avoid being constrained by your own.

Leverage permits you to accumulate more money than you could attain on yourself alone by employing resources other than your own. It enables you to accumulate riches without being constrained by personal constraints.

Leverage is the concept that distinguishes people who achieve money from those who do not. It's as easy as that. If you don't use leverage, you're working more to earn less than you should — and it won't get you rich.

Fourth Principle: Live With Complete Honesty.

Never do or say anything that might embarrass your parents. Don't hurt the environment, create injury, break moral laws or trespass on the property of others. Do not cheat, offend, or lie in your quest for financial gain. *Don't even try to stretch the truth. It's simply not worth it.*

Fifth Principle: Create Friendly Environments.

If accumulating wealth was simple, more people would do so. Even though everyone may devise a fair strategy to get wealthy, few people achieve financial independence. The distinction is based on concentrated action, persistence, and consistency. Life delivers a constant supply of diversions that derail your wealth-building efforts.

The solution is to build a system that ensures you remain on course and practically attracts you toward prosperity. Your daily rituals, relationships, family environment, financial habits, job environment, and other factors must all be proactive to physically pull you toward riches by supporting and reinforcing your objectives.

You must arrange your life to achieve financial success. It's the road with the least amount of opposition. You can either structure your everyday life to achieve your objectives or let your days be filled with options.

Sixth Principle: Be Disciplined.

Wealth results from many small things added up and compounded over a lifetime. That is to say; your everyday behaviors will either create or ruin your success. Investing, saving, reinvesting, and expanding your business and financial knowledge are all important wealth-building practices that need regular and steady work.

In other words, wealth creation necessitates ***discipline***.

Without discipline, you risk succumbing to the number one money destroyer: procrastination. You must start developing good habits right now. Starting now and continuing tomorrow requires discipline to overcome procrastination.

There is no replacement for action. Anything less is only an explanation.

"Magical thinking" is another impediment to developing regular everyday routines. The mistaken notion is that financial stability will materialize out of thin air without any precise strategy or activity. Wealth happens because you put forth the effort to make it happen. The impression of "instant wealth" results from years of dedicated, everyday behaviors because luck favors those who create opportunities.

Seventh Principle: Have Courage

Humans are social animals; therefore, we are hesitant to venture out independently. However, prosperity does not come from just following the majority. It is the outcome of doing what others will not do to obtain what others will never have. Being a self-starter and self-responsible demands bravery. It requires bravery and guts to venture down new roads, learn new talents, and stand out in a crowd. In addition, going the extra mile requires bravery, especially when others won't.

To summarize, building wealth requires ***courage***. Live with courage so that you can live completely and enjoy genuine prosperity.

Eighth Principle: Avoid Conspicuous Consumption

The allure of a "more, better, different" lifestyle is the false carrot for accumulating money. Wealth, in truth, is a type of delayed gratification. People who are focused on building wealth spend less, live within their means, and invest more.

They recognize that satisfaction does not come from worldly possessions, for doing so would simply prohibit them from satisfying the deeper reason that pushes them to succeed.

Every day, you must choose between today's consumption and tomorrow's riches. If your cause is a lifestyle, spending takes precedence, rendering money unattainable.

Wealth Secrets The Rich Won't Tell You

Chapter THREE

Wealth-Building Mistakes to Avoid

There is a distinction between being wealthy and creating wealth. It takes time to accumulate money. You must be both patient and always take advantage of opportunities. Furthermore, you must avoid typical blunders that can derail your quest. That being stated, if you wish to acquire wealth, avoids the following four money mistakes:

1. Diversification

If you want to perfect something, you must put in the time. Take real estate as an example. To become a great real estate magnate, you must first study everything you can about the industry. Remember that you may always diversify your assets within a single portfolio. Diversification does not imply investing in every industry or opportunity. Simply study and fully understand all the key details about a particular sector before diving in, head first.

2. Depending Solely on Your Salary

The golden rule of wealth creation is to generate many revenue sources. If you rely only on your wage for income, you are limiting your earning possibilities. You must develop passive revenue streams.

Real estate, for example, is an excellent method to generate passive income. If you don't want to buy real estate, check out these 11 methods to generate money while sleeping. Start by selecting one that matches your schedule and skill set.

3. Maintaining a Savings Accounts

To be blunt, you cannot grow money only by saving. Savings accounts, in particular, do not generate enough returns. Most banks give 0.25 per cent yearly interest on savings accounts. That implies that it will take forty years to double your money by 10%. I can practically promise you'll generate more than 0.25 per cent annual returns on your money if you perform adequate research and design an investment strategy.

4. Trusting Others without Question

Blindly following the counsel of others is one of the most costly financial blunders you can make. It's easy to trust those who have come before you. However, investment is extremely dangerous, and there is no such thing as a 100 per cent guarantee (generally speaking). Never, regardless of their status, put your faith in someone. Always conduct your research and make sound conclusions.

Simple Money Habits for Wealth Building in the Future

Building wealth for the future ultimately boils down to forming a few habits. There are several financial habits that everyone may adopt to develop long-term wealth. While no one can tell you how to build your portfolio exactly, here are some broad recommendations and practices you may adopt to make your future more profitable:

1. Keep track of your spending.

You can't accumulate wealth if more money leaves your wallet than comes in. Track your everyday costs to verify you're earning more than you spend. Level Money, Personal Capital, and Mint are just a few applications that will accomplish this for you.

You can keep track of your daily purchases in a notepad, on your phone, or use a spreadsheet on your computer.

2. Make your finances more automated.

If your financial strategy isn't on autopilot, it should be. You may easily grow wealth by automating your finances or directing your money to savings and investment accounts. Connect your accounts in a way that funds received via your paycheck automatically goes to your savings account. You can make adjustments and chose the days you wish to make these transfers and automate them. In addition to never being late again, automation frees up vital time.

3. Surround yourself with people who make a lot of money.

Who you interact with matters more than you would ever know. In reality, your net worth closely resembles that of your closest pals. Successful individuals often feel that success is contagious and that exposure to more successful people can broaden your thinking and propel your income.

4. Put your "spare coins" to good use.

Investing is one of the most successful methods to accumulate wealth, and contrary to common assumptions, it does not require a large sum of money to start. Indeed, micro-investment applications allow you to begin by just investing your "spare change."

These apps round up your expenditures to the next dollar and puts any spare cash to good use. Other applications try to make investing more accessible and straightforward, and automated investment services may operate for you regardless of your financial balance.

5. Read for 30 minutes every day.

Rich folks read a lot. They focus on teaching and investing, even after conventional schooling has ended. Among the first features you'll discover when you enter into the home of a wealthy individual is a vast collection of books they've used to enlighten themselves on becoming more successful. It may work for you if it works for millionaires and billionaires.

6. Establish clear financial objectives.

One main reason why many individuals don't get what they desire is because they don't set clear goals or objectives. Rich individuals are unequivocal in their desire for riches. Consider setting down your annual income and net worth objectives to get that degree of clarity. Be realistic in your goal-setting, but don't be afraid to push yourself. After all, the wealthy aren't scared to dream large.

7. Tell yourself that you deserve to be wealthy.

The most prosperous people feel that pleasure, prosperity, and contentment are the natural order of things. This one idea motivates the exceptional ones to act in ways that ensure their success. On the other hand, the average earner remains average since it is what they anticipate. The majority of people believe they are unworthy of an enormous fortune.

8. Save unexpected funds rather than spending them.

Pretend the additional money doesn't exist, whether it's a windfall, bonus, or birthday check. Make a practice of putting any unexpected income to work, even if it's only a $20 bill found in your coat pocket. Put it towards a savings account, an emergency fund, or school debt. It will all add up. Furthermore, developing this practice early on can help you prevent lifestyle inflation when you receive additional cash in the form of a raise.

In summary, the following ten essential concepts can help you stay on course when accumulating long-term wealth:

1. **Manage Your Wealth**: Money is only a tool that comes with the obligation to utilize it properly. It's not something you own but flows through you and must be returned.

2. **Handle Your Investment Like A Business:** You are in the money-management industry as a wealth creator, and you must maintain your net worth in the same manner that a good investor does.

3. **Use Leverage**: Leverage distinguishes people who become wealthy from those who do not. You can't get there by exchanging time for money, and you can't accomplish it all by yourself. You require leverage.

4. **Create a Supportive Environment**: Creating supportive environments that physically drive you toward the objective paves the route to prosperity with the least amount of opposition.

5. **Avoid Prominent Consumption**: No one has ever spent their way to financial independence. Every day, you must choose between today's consumption and tomorrow's riches.

6. **Be Disciplined**: So many things happening in life will try to divert your focus away from your main goal. Only the diligent will stick to the plan and take consistent enough action to see results.

7. **Be Courageous:** Wealth is earned by doing what everyone else wouldn't do in order to achieve what everybody else can never have.

8. **Maintain Absolute Integrity:** Honesty is non-negotiable since money cannot buy a proper night's sleep, a strong moral compass, or a peaceful mind.

9. **Give More Than You Take:** When you give more than you take, your financial performance mirrors how much you have given to the world. It's a rewarding way to life.

10. **Create Riches For A Meaningful Purpose**: When you give value, your financial success reflects how much you have contributed to the world. It's a fulfilling way to live.

Wealth Secrets The Rich Won't Tell You

Chapter FOUR

Long-Term Wealth Development Strategies

How can someone accumulate wealth that would last a long time? I'm certain that you would like to know how; but first, you have to understand what 'wealth' is all about. So, first and foremost, what precisely is wealth? Wealth is a substantial quantity of valuable assets, properties, and monetary gains. Let us first define the distinction between wealthy and rich. For a brief time, one can be wealthy.

You can get rich by hitting the jackpot, becoming a professional athlete or entertainer, or becoming a business owner. But the money would be gone if you lose your earning ability. And you won't be handing down anything to future generations. A rich individual, on the other hand, possesses long-term wealth. Wealthy individuals, in reality, know how to generate money.

You know what; education and constancy are the keys to prosperity. You can create long-term riches if you have knowledge and consistency. Otherwise, you may get wealthy, but the wealth is unlikely to endure. To return to the million-dollar issue, how can you create long-term wealth?

So, let's look at some long-term wealth-creation strategies:

1. Tax Preparation

Many people actually believe that anyone earning more is liable to pay an equivalent in taxes. But this school of thought isn't quite true, especially if you have a structure and plan in place for tax payments. You can use an equity-linked savings program to save taxes (ELSS). It offers tax benefits as well as the chance of higher earnings than traditional tax-saving options such as Fixed Deposit, Public Provident Fund, and National Provident Scheme.

We've seen a variety of money-growing strategies, but keep in mind that in order to build wealth; you would have to have a long-term approach. Short-term strategies will not produce the intended results. Also, investing in yourself is the best decision you can take on securing your financial future. Make it a habit to upgrade and strengthen your spirit and talents to help you in making better decisions to accumulating wealth.

2. Set a Financial goal for yourself.

Your objectives should be explicit and quantifiable. Make a list of your objectives that you may refer to remind you of them regularly. Your objective may be to buy a house, support your children's education, purchase a car, or travel worldwide. Remember that planning ahead of time guarantees that you have enough time to reach your financial objectives.

3. Begin Investing

Savings are insufficient. You must start investing right away. Once you've established a financial plan and saved enough money, you should begin investing; selecting the correct combination of assets is crucial. Putting too much or too little money into a single asset might lead to liquidity problems. Fixed deposits, equities, bonds, real estate, gold, and collective investment schemes are a few of the investing alternatives accessible.

Investments are a sure-fire approach to amass a substantial portfolio in a few years while increasing your net worth over time. It is also simple to handle because the research and fund management choose the finest assets. It is also simple to buy because several secure platforms are available. Select one solid large-cap fund and one strong mid-cap fund to reduce risk.

4. Make saving a priority.

Ever wondered how much funds you should save or set aside for future purpose. Some suggest 30% of one's annual wage, while others say 50%. That depends on your objectives. However, disciplined saving can help you avoid numerous mistakes and challenges in life.

5. Develop a sound financial strategy.

A financial strategy is vital after you have settled on a financial objective. It provides a well-defined route to follow to reach your life's objectives. A budget plan helps you manage your money by tracking your taxes, expenses, and savings. And this, in turn, aids you in achieving your financial goals.

Best Kept 'Riches' Secrets That Will Shock You

Indulging in excess spending is a frequent problem for high-income workers, even though they make so much money. They feel that they need to flaunt their money and enjoy it, which frequently leads to excess.

People sometimes fail to grasp that instead of spending their money as it comes in, they may put their money to work by investing and collecting passive income from those assets. The sweet spot is when you have your money working for you and creating even more money.

In no particular order, the best-kept secrets to becoming wealthy are:

1. Create a strategy for success.

The most important secret of all is to have a plan. An objective without proper strategies is simply a desire; therefore map out your expenditures to help you meet your financial targets. It is simpler to measure your progress and keep yourself accountable when you prepare and lay out your goals. A plan makes your goals attainable.

2. Avoid investing in depreciable assets.

Vehicles are the most expensive depreciable asset that people purchase. It's tempting to buy a beautifully branded, fully stocked luxury automobile that will set you back at least six figures. Nonetheless, that money would be better invested and paid back to you.

3. Your net worth is determined by your financial activities.

How you manage your finances, including savings, spending, and investments determine your financial situation. One thing that the most prosperous people have in common is that they are not showy about their wealth. They have a lot of money but don't live an extravagant lifestyle, wear flashy clothes, or vacation on the most expensive yachts.

4. Never spend more than you earn.

It's much easier to spend money on stuff you don't really need, luxury items, gadgets, or even keeping up with the Joneses. But bear it in mind that spending more than you earn is a quick way to accrue countless debts for yourself. Investing in something that pays a return would ensure that your money will be better served.

5. Monitor your net worth while investing.

The greatest approach to gauge your wealth is to keep track of your net worth. Hence, you stand the chance of becoming wealthier as your net worth increases. The things you own, such as investments, rental properties, and anything else with long-term worth, represent your wealth.

6. Invest in financial education.

The financial return is great when you invest in yourself and learn to handle your money, as long as you're putting what you've acquired over the years into practice. When you employ the financial skills you've learned to manage your money properly, you'll see a great return on investment for years to come.

7. Compound interest is the world's eighth marvel.

Your money expands when you gain interests from your numerous investments. When you are in debt, though, the opposite is the case.

Wealth Secrets The Rich Won't Tell You

Chapter FIVE

What exactly is generational wealth?

Generational wealth simply refers to the riches, properties, and huge sums of money (also known as legacy or family wealth) passed down from one generation to the other. Of course, you can leave several valuables and other material things behind for your family, including a healthy DNA and fond memories. However, I'm talking about the financial riches you're able to leave behind. This wealth can take numerous forms, such as financial knowledge, stock market investments, or future real estate holdings.

What is the significance of generational wealth?

If you are beginning from scratch with your money or have a huge debt burden, you should understand the significance of generational wealth. As you progress through your financial adventure, you've probably realized that it's not always simple to recoup from financial blunders.

The more you consider your financial situation, the more you appreciate the importance of generational wealth. If you plan to procreate or already have children or, you may begin to consider their financial destiny. Remember that brown and black families lag behind white families regarding generational wealth-building, as a result of the racial wealth disparity. Building generational wealth is therefore considerably more important if you are a minority.

Generational Wealth: Building from Scratch

Amassing generational wealth is a simple notion. Simply buy assets or save money you do not intend to consume in retirement, so that after your demise, you will have left something tangible for your children and grandchildren. Although, this is easier said than done. Saving for the next generation might seem daunting if you try to grow your finances. That is entirely understandable!

Before preparing for generational wealth, you must establish your retirement savings strategy and other financial goals. Once you grasp your present finances to support your senior years, it is essential to start saving for the future. So, how should you begin saving for generational wealth?

Below are typical scenarios on how to leave a wealthy legacy for your generations unborn.

1. Start with yourself.

Saving for the future is the first essential step to take towards for building wealth that would last for generations. Paying yourself first is the simplest method to save more money. For example, you can choose to deposit the money into your savings account or invest in tangible assets immediately you receive your paycheck.

Inculcating this behavior enables you to grow your savings much faster, and reduce extravagant spending in the process. You should carefully consider investing part of your money to achieve a larger return and, as a result, generate long-term wealth.

2. Create several income sources.

When it comes to how to develop generational wealth, having numerous sources of income can help. The average millionaire has seven revenue sources! There are many different types of income, but one of the greatest is passive income. Active income is earned when you exchange your time for money, such as through a job or a side hustle.

Passive income is earned from your assets after the basic setup takes little effort, like buying and renting out properties, writing books, publishing and earning royalties, and peer-to-peer lending, and so forth are examples. So you must put in the first effort, but after that is done, you will continue to profit from your efforts.

3. Instruct your children on personal finance.

It is believed that 70% of a family's wealth is lost in the second generation, while 90% of the rest dwindles significantly by the time the third generation lays hands on them! With figures like those, it may appear futile to save for a rich legacy. However, financial education may prevent generational wealth loss in many circumstances. After all, if your children lack financial literacy, it is simple to lose generational wealth.

That's akin to asking your child to maintain a classic vintage automobile after you die without teaching them mechanical skills. The automobile would almost certainly break down at some point.

Similarly, if you educate your children nothing about personal finance, the money you leave for them will probably shrink during their lifetime. Because you're interested in handing along family money, you're probably familiar with personal finance. It's your responsibility to educate your children on how money works. This understanding will be the most effective strategy to create and safeguard generational wealth.

There are several approaches you may use when discussing money with your children. You may teach youngsters about money through books, activities, or by allowing them to listen as you discuss financial decisions.

You may even assist children in opening their bank accounts at a young age to emphasize the value of saving for the future.

4. Invest in your child's education.

Investing in your child's education is a great way to build generational wealth and put them up for financial success! Education can often give a means for your children to sustain themselves. Many people with a college degree have the option to seek high-paying employment that can assist them in managing their own money.

Anyone who has received an education will always have that education. Although other things in life come and go, no one can take your education away from you. If you can assist your children in graduating from college debt-free, you are helping to prepare them for a better financial future than many of their peers. Consider how much financial stress you will be able to relieve on your children's shoulders by being able to pay for their education.

5. Make use of life insurance

Life insurance allows you to safeguard your family during your untimely death. A lack of insurance can put your children into less-than-ideal financial situations if you do not earn a living. If you make an effort to invest in a life insurance policy, you may save your children from financial ruin.

Furthermore, if they lose you, they will already deal with a lot.

Don't know what kind of life insurance to get for your family? Take our free course to learn more about life insurance and how you can use it to protect your family's financial future.

6. Create a legacy business.

More than 30 per cent of family-owned firms migrate to the second generation, indicating that they have the potential for significant success. Consider handing over the keys to a thriving firm to your children. Although not all family companies survive to the second generation, yours may. If your hobbies and talents match those of your children, they will likely wish to take over the firm you develop.

You should involve your child in the business from an early age to increase the chances of a successful transfer. They must understand how the business works and how to succeed. If they show little interest in the company you've developed, don't expect them to take over. If they are unable or unwilling to take over the operations, you may want to explore selling the company to fund generational wealth in another way.

7. Invest in real estate

Real estate is another important way to accumulate wealth over time. Real estate may be a solid road to riches since it has the potential for consistent income flows and growing values over time.

The prospect of constructing a real estate empire might be scary. But it doesn't have to be that way! You may have entered the real estate market by obtaining a mortgage to purchase your first house. You might be amazed at how rapidly your real estate portfolio can develop if you continue acquiring homes once a time throughout your life.

8. Invest in the stock market.

Long-term wealth creation may be accomplished through the stock market. If you want to create generational wealth, it is an excellent alternative because it can increase for decades. It may seem intimidating if you've never invested in the stock market. It is, nevertheless, a crucial strategy to develop money during your lifetime and beyond.

If you are new to the stock market, the best place to begin is with low-cost index funds. These funds can provide cheap fees as well as long-term growth.

Wealth Secrets The Rich Won't Tell You

Chapter SIX

Ways of Building Wealth from Scratch

Attempting to generate wealth from nothing may appear to be a "mission impossible," especially if you've ever imagined that wealthy people acquired their fortunes or gained from major connections. Today, rather of fantasizing about the money you wish you had received, we highly advise you to learn how to build a fortune from nothing.

Here are eight tangible measures **you can take right now** to start building wealth from scratch and enjoying a more financially free lifestyle.

1. Embrace passive investment.

To amass wealth, you should first think about saving and then investing. If you followed the steps above, you should now be saving at least 20% of your salary and earning more through various side hustles. Now is the moment to combine the two and begin investing substantially.

All the billionaires you know and respect amassed their riches via lucrative and prudent stock market investments. If you don't earn enough money to complete the labor, you'll have to do it anyhow. The problem is that your earning capacity is limited, and you can't make money while sleeping (as Buffett advised).

For starters, putting money in a bank account isn't even an investment. You should only retain money in your emergency reserve. Aside from all of that, your money can be invested in profitable companies that offer significant returns while minimizing risk.

2. Become financially educated.

Before we can genuinely address any bigger improvements in our life, we must constantly change our thinking. Everyone possesses the innate ability to prosper and survive by building a financial ark that can withstand economic turbulence. To build an ark with a solid foundation, you should first invest more time in your financial knowledge.

The first step to take towards becoming financially educated and building wealth out of nothing is by spending quality time in your personal finance.

Learn the meanings of key concepts such as expenditures, net worth, income, passive income, financial independence, and return on investment.

Follow financial blogs, read books, attend classes, and listen to podcasts and interviews. Remember that financial education must be ongoing like any other type of education. Never, ever stop learning. Follow only credible blogs that give genuine information and point you to resources from respectable and successful investors, company owners, and financial experts.

3. Investigate potential sources of passive income.

In addition to growing your income through your profession or business, you should look at ways to make passive money. In contrast to your work or business, passive income is revenue you create that does not demand your constant presence or activity.

Passive income is essential for us to learn how to create wealth from scratch. There are two sorts of passive income: passive investment income, in which your money does all of the work, and noninvestment passive income, in which you do some side work.

There are several methods to make money and build wealth in today's digital and dynamic economy. However, when investigating these prospects, be aware of get-rich-quick schemes such as Ponzi schemes and gambling websites.

Some tried-and-true passive income concepts include:

- **Drop shipping:** Drop shipping involves selling products from other merchants without needing to keep inventory of those items yourself. When a consumer places an order with you, you process it with the producer, who delivers it to the customer. Your income is the difference between the retail and purchase prices.

- **Affiliate marketing**: Rather than selling your own digital products, you can sell products belonging to other vendors and receive a commission upon every sale. Affiliate marketing eliminates the requirement for you to develop your product.

- **Blogging:** Rather than selling your concept as a digital product, you may offer it in the form of a series of regular blog articles. Once your blog has enough traffic, you may monetize it through guest articles, Google AdSense, sponsorships, digital items, and paid membership, among other methods.

- **Selling digital items/products**: If you are a specialist in a specific field, produce digital products on themes that people are interested in. Paid webinars, eBooks, email courses, and video courses are examples of digital goods. The benefit of digital items is that they only need to be created once, except for future upgrades. You can make lots of money from a single digital product for a long period.

4. Establish a consistent source of income

Without a consistent source of income, it is difficult to create wealth from scratch. You can't afford to invest unless you focus on saving money, therefore you can't save money unless you already have a steady income. This suggests that individuals do not acquire long-term riches through gambling, multilevel marketing, or Ponzi schemes.

Learn to ignore those who promote get-rich-quick schemes that really need only three hours of work each week. Long-term value development produces long-term prosperity. It is difficult to create long-term wealth if you are not creating intrinsic value and collecting money from that thing or service. Continue to focus on building more long-term value if you operate a small firm. All money is created through adding value, which involves developing a company strategy capable of "producing more, cheaper, better, simpler, and faster outcomes."

5. Expand your skill set

You may boost your investments and savings by increasing your income or decreasing your spending. At the same time, many financial counselors concentrate on the latter, the former merits equal consideration. Attend professional classes and immerse yourself in ongoing career progression to expand your skills and experience as an employee.

You can receive promotions or better job offers from other firms by increasing your abilities (both hard and soft), which equals more money. If you own a small firm, you can further improve your market knowledge by providing your customers with more value and spending more money on innovation. You can also grow your market share and income by doing so.

6. Make a budget

Making and sticking to a budget is critical if you hope to learn and understand the various ways of building wealth from scratch. Using the consistent revenue source we discussed, you must now develop a budget to control how you spend your money, normally set monthly.

A budget is an estimation that contains predicted income and spending for a specific time period. Every person or household should develop a monthly budget to specify planned expenditures and revenue. Living without a good budget is like sailing without some kind of compass, and you'll end yourself lost in the oceans of financial mistakes.

7. Create an emergency fund.

After mapping out a proper budget and planning your savings, the next step will be to establish an emergency fund system. An emergency fund works in the same way as self-funded insurance does. It might be money for unexpected needs like auto repairs or unforeseen events like job loss or pandemic-induced lockdowns.

An emergency fund, like reimbursement, will not make you a millionaire, but it will save you from liquidating your assets or incurring debt in the event of emergency situations.

8. Have adequate insurance

Insurance is a necessary expenditure that you should budget for. Insuring yourself and all your major assets protects you against big losses in the event of an accident. At the very least, you should get health insurance to avoid financial ruin in the unfortunate case of an expensive condition. Whether you have children or dependant relatives, you should consider obtaining term life insurance.

Building wealth is enjoyable, but losing it due to unexpected conditions and occurrences is excruciating. So take the initiative and safeguard what you love and rightfully own. However, don't over-insure. Several insurance products are available on the market that are utterly useless. Unless there is a compelling need to obtain additional, stick to the four above.

Purchasing insurance does not change your life, but it does keep your life from changing. You would not become bankrupt as a result of getting insurance, but if you do not, your family members will.

Wealth Secrets The Rich Won't Tell You

BONUS

Passive Income Ideas for Future Wealth

Passive income generates unearned residual revenue while requiring little time and effort. It can help you better your finances and grant you ample time. Not having to sell your time for money might lessen stress and anxiety while increasing your financial confidence.

Increasing your passive income streams can give you more money, independence, and flexibility. Discover 13 methods to generate passive income, with examples and how to get started right away:

1. Buying and selling websites.

There are websites on almost any topic you can think of. What's the best part? Many earn a good living through affiliates, advertisements, subscriptions, or products—they're frequently for sale. It's an excellent method to own a business that already has some revenue and traffic. After you finish your purchase, you will have access to seller assistance to help you succeed.

2. Provide online services.

Online service provider now offer online courses using software and techniques that makes the whole process a lot easier. You may design and sell courses with little restrictions, whether it's entrepreneurship, marketing, or illustration. Online courses, like digital items, can be sold frequently without needing inventory or stock. Teaching online necessitates an initial time investment. You must outline the course, record it, and create digital assets such as templates for students to take away.

3. Earn money by shopping online.

When you purchase online, you may earn money through cashback reward programs. After joining up, you don't have to do anything else to make money from these sites. And making more money always feels better money, especially when shopping at your favorite mall. A word of caution: don't max up your credit card or go over your monthly spending budget to collect a reward.

4. Start a blog.

It might be tough to start a blog, but the blogging business strategy is becoming more and more popular as a passive money source. You don't have to be an internet celebrity to make money online these days. You must identify your target audience on one or two social media platforms and drive them to your website. Building a blog takes time and work. However, if you create high-quality content and distribute it across your platforms, you will build a large enough audience to benefit.

5. Set up a YouTube channel.

Setting up a YouTube channel isn't too late since over 74.5 percent of adults in the United States use YouTube. That's a lot of prospective consumers to snare for passive income. What's the snag? YouTube offers the chance of earning passive income with minimal effort and commitment. A successful YouTube channel has great earning potential. Ad revenue, affiliate sales, branded integrations, and sponsorships may build up quietly as your audience grows, views, content, and clicks collect.

6. Run an affiliate marketing company.

Affiliate marketing is the practice of suggesting a service or product to a certain demographic. It's a terrific way to generate passive money since you get paid every time someone clicks on your referral link and purchases the suggested goods or service. It is also a booming business, with a projected value of $28.2 billion by 2030.

7. Invest in the stock market.

When it comes to stock investment, most people consider the short to medium term instead of just the long term. The purpose of stock investing is to lower risk and diversify your portfolio. You can accomplish this by investing in high-dividend equities and exchange-traded funds, which provide income gradually over time. To finally start investing in stocks, you must first open and establish a brokerage account.

8. Become an Instagram influencer.

To become an Instagram influencer, you must first develop a network of individuals interested in similar themes. If you like comic books, you may create an Instagram account and post about the latest DC and Marvel programs. The same holds for general culture, sports, home décor, or even scuba diving.

9. Market digital products.

Because of their huge profit margins, digital items are excellent passive income sources. You simply need to create the asset once, and you may sell it several times online. There is no need for storage or inventory. Stream able or downloadable files such as PDFs, Kindle novels, plug-ins, or templates are examples of assets or pieces of media that consumers cannot physically touch.

10. Record audiobooks.

Once established in the business, you may earn passive money from recording audiobooks. To make a living off audiobooks, you must first learn how to edit, audition, the niche you'll work in, and suitable narrating methods.

11. Online design sales.

Design websites may be excellent platforms for selling digital creations online. Whether you utilize a website builder to create logos, website themes, branding resources, fonts, drawings, or even templates, these platforms provide an already-existing market for design materials.

12. Create a digital product.

You most likely have extensive knowledge on a subject others are eager to pay for. Try putting your expertise to use by creating digital manuals. There is little barrier to entry, and in many situations, no money is required to get started. What you need to invest is time as it is what you'll need to scour around and find what people need the most. Google recommendations might be an excellent starting point.

13. Sell NFTs.

NFTs or Non-fungible tokens are unique assets recorded on a digital ledger. The benefit of NFTs is that the asset stored can be valuable. NFTs may be made for anything, such as films, digital designs, GIFs, photography, games, and music. It is simple to set up an NFT. Create an account on sites like OpenSea and follow the step-by-step minting process.

Wealth Secrets The Rich Won't Tell You

Conclusion

Wealth implies different things to different individuals, regardless matter how wealthy they are. For some, that means paying for all of their children's college educations. Others define riches as the opportunity to rest all day, large residences, and flashy automobiles. Regardless of what you think wealth is, budgeting is the first critical step in creating long-term prosperity.

Long-term wealth creation is truly feasible for everyone. It all starts with having ideas and making financial plans. You will never be able to achieve your goals unless you have a clear plan and a strong concentration. The first stage in accumulating wealth is to establish five priorities. For example, if you are unhappy with your present living arrangement, you may set a goal of putting $10,000 down payment on a house in six years.

These objectives should also contain a time period for when you want to be financially secure. Knowing what path you want to pursue and remaining organized implies that money creation is part of the bigger plan. It will not only push you to work harder, but it will also help you to glimpse what is ahead. The following step is to construct a budget. Wealth creation does not happen by itself, thus you must sit down and maintain track of your finances. You will easily achieve your objective if you create a budget and stick to it.

Many financial experts advocate maintaining a diary and a financial list. That way, you can see what you're saving. Keep the receipts and perform the arithmetic if you go to the grocery shop twice a week, for example. If you start to have doubts, just consider the eventual outcome. Would you prefer to squander $100 weekly on unhealthy food or save enough for a home in ten years? As long as you stick to your rules, the possibilities are limitless.

You must research extra facts once you have defined a budget, a goal, and a timeframe. Every financial analyst wishes to be financially secure in the long run. They may learn what and how to avoid and what to try by attending money creation workshops. It is frequently tough to begin such a major endeavor when you are in debt or just do not know where to begin. Looking into a real estate investment seminar might also be beneficial for folks who are just starting to pay their mortgage.

While long-term wealth planning is difficult, money creation is not a distant fantasy for most people.

Denise J. Whalen

Progress and adjustments are possible as long as your goals and budget are reasonable, and you remain positive.